INSPIRATIONAL TREASURES

Published in the United States by
Beckham Publications Group, Inc.
P.O. Box 4066, Silver Spring, MD 20914

ISBN: 0-9848243-9-7

INSPIRATIONAL TREASURES

Essays by Educators and Students Reflecting the Joys of Teaching

DISTRICT OF COLUMBIA RETIRED EDUCATORS ASSOCIATION, INC.

WWW.DCREA.NET

COMPILED BY
CHRISTINE DAVIS EASTERLING
FRANCES GREEN CLARKE

EDITED BY
THELMA AUSTIN/PRAISE PRESS

Beckham
PUBLICATIONS GROUP, INC.

Silver Spring

These treasures praising the joy and excitement of teaching are dedicated to the founders and past presidents of the District of Columbia Retired Teachers Association (now District of Columbia Retired Educators Association).

This first published title should inspire and encourage retired educators everywhere to write and publish their own stories.

Greetings—

District of Columbia Retired Educators Association, Inc.
Book Writing Club

May 2011

As Mayor of the District of Columbia, it is my pleasure to extend congratulations to the District of Columbia Retired Educators Association, Inc., Book Writing Club, on the occasion of your first book release entitled: *Inspirational Treasures for Educators.*

This book should serve as an inspiration to retired educators and encourage them to write their own books. Writings will include inspirational messages, poems, prayers, teacher experiences, essays, and much more. As you gather to celebrate this special occasion, we look forward to future publications.

On behalf of the residents of the District of Columbia, you have my best wishes for an enjoyable event.

Vincent C. Gray
Mayor, District of Columbia

CONTENTS

STUDENTS' EXPRESSIONS OF PRAISE   61

ABOUT THE AUTHORS (EDUCATORS)   93

EPILOGUE   103

Acknowledgments

The following persons were indispensable to the mission and development of this publication. Your support is truly appreciated.

Members of the District of Columbia Retired Educators Association, Inc. (DCREA)

DCREA Book Writing Club Members and Authors:

Frances Green Clarke
Alberta R. Clément
Emma J. Coates
Alberta H. Coleman
Christine D. Easterling
Phyllis J. Hobson
Minnie L. Holcomb
Sandra Britt Jenkins
Constance T. Laws

Louise M. Mikell
Delore President
Marie Richardson
Ermyn Roberts
William H. Simons
Shirley A. Smith
Romaine B. Thomas
Jacqueline S. Williams
Marion O. Williams

Raymond Education Campus, Washington, D.C.

Natalie Hubbard, Principal
Tonya Williams, Vice Principal
Rhonda Scott, Teacher (5th Grade)
Cassandra Wilkins, Teacher (4th Grade)
Esan Fullington, Aftercare Coordinator
Brenda Manley, Administrative Assistant
Other Teachers and Staff
Student Authors

The Honorable Vincent C. Gray
Mayor, District of Columbia

The Honorable Arne Duncan
Secretary, U. S. Department of Education

Thelma Austin/Praise Press
Editor

Epigraphs

"If you want to make a difference in the life of our nation; if you want to make a difference in the life of a child . . . become a teacher. Your country needs you."

–President Barack Obama
State of the Union Speech
January 25, 2011

"In fact, new evidence shows that from the moment our children step into a classroom, the single most important factor in determining their achievement is not the color of their skin or where they come from; it's not who their parents are or how much money they have. It's who their teacher is. It's you."

"It's you who can reach the most challenging students. It's you who will stay past the last bell and spend your own money on books and supplies. It's you who will go beyond the call because you believe that's what makes the extra difference. And it does."

–President Barack Obama
July 5, 2007

"Most teachers will tell you that the rewards of being a teacher far outstrip its disappointments. Teaching is one of the few professions that are not just a job or even an adventure—it's a calling. It is mission-driven work. Great teachers strive to help every student unlock their potential and develop the habits of mind that will serve them for a lifetime. They believe that every student has a gift—even when students doubt themselves."

"There is a reason why so many of us remember a favorite teacher, even decades later. A great teacher can literally change the course of a student's life. They light a lifelong curiosity, stoke a hunger for learning, and teach self-discipline and grit. The teachers that you will remember years later are the ones who wanted you to solve problems like a scientist, write like a poet, see like an artist, and observe like a journalist."

–U.S. Secretary of Education Arne Duncan
"The Lasting Impact of Teachers"
Lesley University Commencement Speech
May 19, 2010

"Great teachers are the unsung heroes in our society. They have the single biggest in-school impact on academic achievement. And when it comes to teaching, commitment, love for the work, and talent matter tremendously."

–U.S. Secretary of Education Arne Duncan
Speech at World Bank
March 3, 2011

PREFACE

History shows that in the early 1900s, one teacher would teach five to eight grade levels and all subjects. The female teachers, most of whom were unmarried, would arrive very early to start a fire in the pot belly stove, prepare hot meals for the students, and clean their classrooms. All this was in addition to their usual duties of preparing lessons and grading papers.

Teachers rarely earned any significant recognition or income. The average monthly wages for a female teacher in a "one-room school" was $25.99.

When I think of our educators, I am reminded of the poem by Ivan Welton Fitzwater who in 2008 received the American Association of School Administrators Distinguished Service Award:

> *I am a teacher! What I do and say are being absorbed by young minds who will echo these images across the ages. My lessons will be immortal, affecting people yet unborn, people I will never see or know.*
>
> *The future of the world is in my classroom today, a future with the potential for good or bad. The pliable minds of tomorrow's leaders will be molded either artistically or grotesquely by what I do. Several future presidents are learning from me today; so are the great writers of the next decades; and so are all the so-called ordinary people who will make the decisions in a democracy.*
>
> *I must never forget these same young people could be the thieves or murderers of the future. Only a teacher? Thank God I have a calling to the greatest profession of all! I must be vigilant every day lest I lose one fragile opportunity to improve tomorrow.*

In September 2010, as president of the District of Columbia Retired Educators Association, I encouraged the organization to establish a book writing club. The ultimate purpose of the club is to encourage retired educators to write their own books. It was our hope that when educators read our first collaborative book, *Inspirational Treasures: Essays by Educators and Students Reflecting the Joys of Teaching,* they would feel appreciated and proud of choosing education as their profession.

Inspirational Treasures: Essays by Educators and Students Reflecting the Joys of Teaching features inspirational messages, poems, prayers, teacher experiences, short stories, acrostics, essays, meditations, and more from the members. In addition, the book includes praises from students in the second through seventh grades at Raymond Education Campus. We hope that this book will live forever in the hearts and minds of educators everywhere—to remind them not only how great they are, but also how great their contributions to society have been.

Christine D. Easterling

DISTRICT OF COLUMBIA RETIRED EDUCATORS ASSOCIATION, INC.

(formerly District of Columbia Retired Teachers Association, Inc.)

Historical Overview

Louise M. Mikell, Archivist: 2010-2012
Alberta Clément, Archivist: 2008-2010
Marie Richardson, Archivist: 2006-2008

Our Beginning

The District of Columbia Retired Teachers Association (DCRTA) was founded in 1955 by retired teachers May P. Bradshaw and Corrine Martin for the "benefit and mutual pleasure of its members." In 1956, Ms. Bradshaw served as the first president and Ms. Martin was elected vice president. The membership worked to improve annuities to keep pace with COLAS and

health care costs. An office was opened at Roosevelt High School. Committees were organized to write the constitution and bylaws.

Throughout the years, DCRTA has maintained its focus on legislative needs and benefits for retired educators while providing workshops for members and services for the community.

Presidents of DCRTA (DCREA as of 2010)

1956-1957	May P. Bradshaw	1984-1986	Beverly Carrell
1957-1959	Elsie Green	1986-1988	Martha Rogers
1959-1961	Charles Foster	1988-1990	Sarah P. Moore
1961-1963	Margaret Moore	1990-1992	Jennie B. White
1963-1965	Ellis Haworth	1992-1994	Talmadge L. Moore
1965-1966	Winfred McNeill	1994-1996	Elsie C. Mitchell
1966-1968	Anita Blake	1996-1998	Alicemarie Pitts
1968-1970	Charles Bish	1998-2000	Alma P. Felder
1970-1972	Mary Keehka	2000	Althea W. Bethel
1972-1974	Madison W. Tignor	2000-2004	Paula B. McKann
1974-1976	Elizabeth D. Griffith	2004-2006	Phyllis J. Hobson
1976-1978	E. Fillmore Mitchell	2006-2008	Norman E. Jenkins
1978-1980	Frances R. Mitchell	2008-2010	Phyllis J. Hobson
1980-1982	Wilma J. Shepherd	2010-2012	Christine D. Easterling
1982-1984	Maurice M. Johnson		

Highlights of 1956-1970s

- Participated in efforts for passage of Public Law 648, which raised annuities for retired D.C. government personnel.
- Became affiliated with the National Retired Teachers Association (NRTA) of the American Association for Retired Persons (AARP) to secure insurance, hospital, and pharmaceutical benefits for retired teachers.
- Increased annuities by ten percent through successful lobbying.
- Supported the partnership of DCRTA and NRTA to establish the D.C. joint legislative committee to unify the legislative efforts of NRTA and AARP.

- Encouraged DCRTA representatives to work vigorously for the D.C. police officers, firefighters, teachers and judges' pension bill, which became Public Law 96-122.

Highlights of 1980s

- Supported merger of NRTA and AARP which created the NRTA division.
- DCRTA member E. Fillmore Mitchell elected first representative for retired teachers on the D.C. Retirement Board.
- Presented first scholarship to a senior from a D.C. public high school pursuing a degree in education.
- Presented the DCRTA archives to the Sumner Center for Preservation.
- Became incorporated as the D.C. Retired Teachers Association, Inc.
- Initiated pre-retirement planning seminars.
- Established Golden Membership for active and financial members 85 years of age and older.
- Held first DCRTA Annual Spring Luncheon.
- Conducted the first combined workshop with the members of the AARP Chapters.
- Leadership workshop established for AARP and DCRTA in the national AARP headquarters in Washington.

Highlights of 1990s

- Established "telephone tree" to maintain closer communications with members.
- Conducted Christmas bazaar and health fair for December and March meetings, respectively.
- Sponsored the Community Service Committee, an inter-generational project teaching D.C. public elementary

school children how to assist residents of the Washington Home of Aging.

- President Clinton signed Title IX of the Balanced Budget Act of 1997 (Public Law 105-33), which focused on education and included the "D.C. Protection Act."
- Past President Elsie Mitchell named "Teacher of the Year" on the 50th anniversary of NRTA.

Highlights of 2000-2009

- Increased scholarship funds through generous private donations, drives and projects.
- Acquired site for DCRTA home office for meetings and official storage repository at Raymond Education Campus in Washington.
- Initiated procedures to acquire IRS 501c(3) status.
- Adopted Raymond Education Campus and instituted a system to provide administrative and instructional support services.

Highlights of 2010-2012

- Developed and implemented two-year plan.
- Changed name to District of Columbia Retired Educators Association, Inc. (DCREA) to reflect inclusion of teachers and other educators.
- Revised DCREA logo.
- Created first website: www.dcrea.net
- Participated in AARP's Leadership Conference for officers and chairpersons, strengthening our affiliation with AARP.
- Appointed new committees: music, book writers, awards, public relations, travel, cultural events.
- Took first international group trip (2011 cruise to Bermuda).
- Implemented call post messaging service.

- Commenced printing newsletters in full color. Distribution includes collaborating organizations.
- Instituted "Dance for Your Health" (line dance classes) before each meeting.
- Created White House Writing Project (for students) at Raymond Education Campus.
- Implemented School Supplies Project with AARP.
- Created Annual Founders' Day Tea with Hat Parade.
- Created "New Member Portfolio."
- Published two pictorial summaries: "One-Year in Review" and "Two-Year in Review."
- Published *Inspirational Treasures: Essays by Educators and Students Reflecting the Joys of Teaching*

EDUCATORS'
REFLECTIONS

TEACHING IS AS OLD
AS THE UNIVERSE

William H. Simons

While teaching is as old as the universe, the development of teaching as a profession is a relatively new phenomenon. Young people had to be taught the rudiments of survival. The girls were given instructions by their mothers while the boys were taught by their fathers how to gather food by hunting and later by planting. This was true in colonial America. Girls were taught the rudiments of reading and writing while the boys followed their fathers into the fields.

Education supported by the community had its beginnings in the Colony of Massachusetts when in 1642 a law was passed requiring parents to teach their children how to read. Five years later, the Colony enacted legislation requiring every town of 50 families to start an elementary school and every town of 100 families to start a Latin grammar school.

With the fall of the Greek Empire to the Romans, Greek educators were made slaves and were forced to continue their teaching. Teachers were denigrated for a long time after this change. It wasn't until after the Industrial Revolution that the realization occurred that a different kind of teacher training and more teachers were needed in order to produce the kinds of students needed.

Teachers also began to realize that teaching was becoming a profession the same as medicine and law. As a profession, the practitioners needed to be part of the decision-making process. This led to the formation of organizations which would provide teachers a voice in the decision-making process. As a result, teachers are now a part of the decision-making process in determining their working conditions and how and what is to be taught to their students.

While much progress has been made, much more needs to be done to insure that teachers are truly included in the ranks of the professions.

CELEBRATE EDUCATORS

Dr. Phyllis J. Hobson

❖ They bring forth miracles in the lives of MANY.

❖ Their creative LEADERSHIP directs career paths.

❖ They build relationships based on TRUST.

❖ Their key for enjoying success TODAY is doing it NOW!

❖ They encourage the next generation not to follow, but to OVERTAKE.

Celebrate EDUCATORS
for practicing the most
HONORABLE profession.

A NOBLE CALLING

Jacqueline S. Williams

Not many of you should presume to be teachers, my brothers and sisters, because you know that we who teach will be judged more strictly.

—James 3:1

Whether you are
aspiring to be a teacher,
currently "serving" in a teaching position,
providing support to someone who is teaching,
planning to return to teaching or mentoring,
or writing your memoirs,
it is vital that you remember that what you are called to do is
"A Noble Calling."

Many who have served in these roles for a time, or aspired to serve or observed from the sidelines and found that they were not so called, have been awed at what is required of such "soldiers" and servants of the people. The professional educator—called to serve in this position—must be *"a special human being, always on public display, a role model of ethics—honorable, principled and upright."*

As one who found herself, at an early age, "called" to teach, and who has found that the calling is for a lifetime, I found work during my 45 years as teacher, educational supervisor, director of educational programs and principal to be equally demanding and stimulating. I also found it impossible to live up to the above description expected of us by our public, our parents, our students, other school staff, our community and even, on occasion, our colleagues. While there were innumerable experiences that were exceptionally challenging. I have never regretted accepting—even seeking—the call to teach. I have compassion for others who are so "called." I pray that you will also know and enjoy the rewards of accepting your call and know yourselves to be blessed special people in being so "called."

With the following words in tribute to educators, I humbly but gratefully and joyfully commend all my colleagues who answered the call and have served in the "Noble Profession of Educators."

I honor you for your:

E — ETHICS
Moral principles
That other professions might decry,
But for you and for your children
Your code of values you can't deny.

D — DEVOTION
To duty with your children,
Familiar with their expectant faces;
And their dependence on you to always be
Available in your accustomed places.

U — UNDERSTANDING
Of the minds and needs
Of your little special treasures;
To meet the needs you diagnose
You devise special measures.

C — CHARISMA AND COURAGE
In large measures
Educators must demonstrate
For parents, and colleagues and especially the children
And then you really rate.

A — ATTENTIVENESS

To all kinds of details
And alert to the unexpected;
Always prepared to meet situations
With solutions appropriate and respected.

T — TALENT AND TRUSTWORTHINESS

You wear hats of various sizes and styles
That carry you through the days and weeks
As you walk uncounted school day miles.

O — OPTIMISM

Always required
To carry you all through the day,
To meet the challenges, the ups and downs
Of dealing with a school day

R — RESPONSIBILITY

No problem ever for you,
With the call you knew, of course,
And carried out with exemplary style
No complaint and no remorse.

ADVICE TO A NEW TEACHER

Frances Green Clarke

So you're a new teacher!
Uh-huh!

Be kind.
> *Years later down the road, you'll see a child you taught.*
> *You want this child to say you were kind. Plus, it's the right way*
> *to be.*

Be prepared.
> *Plan! Remember, failure to plan means planned failure.*

Be fair.
> *Fairness will promote respect.*

Be steadfast and firm.
> *These qualities will help you discipline both yourself and others.*

Be curious.
> *And you will spread curiosity.*

Be exploratory.
> *Question all things! Seek the truth in all things!*
> *Dare your students to explore!*
> *This way, you and your students will grow and expand.*

Teach!

So that others may learn.

Be faithful and patient.

Remember, these are virtues, and with them, you can remove roadblocks and mountains!

Be dedicated.

Remember, you are needed to make this world a better place.

And lastly,

"Let your light (in teaching) so shine before men that they may see your good works, glorify your father which is in heaven . . ." and that they may salute this most honorable profession.

THE POWER OF THE SPOKEN WORD

Constance T. Laws

When teachers speak, students listen. In teaching and in every of aspect of life, consider the effect that your words have on others. The effect can last a lifetime.

The spoken word, however uttered,
reveals the thoughts in the human mind,
reveals the beliefs stored within the heart . . .
whether gracious or unkind.

When unspoken, one can only imagine
the cogitation of the soul . . .
Once spoken, there is no retraction
of expressions, whether warm or cold.

So whenever you desire to speak
remember, if voiced, your thought is then heard.
Always use tact, you can't take it back . . .
That's the power of the spoken word.

DIAMONDS IN THE ROUGH

Shirley A. Smith

Successful teachers know that most students succeed because of us, not in spite of us. I am a personal witness from my own youth.

In high school, my mathematics teacher, Mrs. Theresa Oliver, saw in me what I had no idea was in me. She gave me the impression that I possessed strong mathematics potential. She was a no-nonsense teacher. She made me feel so special but laid me out whenever I made a mistake. I was extremely flattered when she assigned me to peer-mentor my classmates. The students began referring to me as SMART (little did they realize that it might mean "Succeed in Math And Respect Teacher"). They would rely on me to help when they had difficulty. Soon I started thinking of myself as a strong math student. As a result, I felt good about myself and succeeded in all of my classes.

Mrs. Oliver patiently polished me like a jeweler works on a diamond in the rough. Consequently, I developed a love for mathematics. I majored in mathematics in college, became a mathematics teacher, and taught for over forty years. I retired from both the District of Columbia Public School System and the Montgomery County, Maryland Public School System. Along the way, I have seen many students' light bulbs turn on in my classes.

In every class, there is a mine full of students—diamonds—in the rough. A student quickly detects your impression of him, then rises (or falls) to your expectations. The teacher must always believe in the student. See each student as unique. Find a positive asset, talent, skill, strength of each one. Help him focus on, develop and strengthen that skill. He must be convinced that you believe in him.

Keep in mind that the student spends more of her waking hours at school than at home. Think of the whole person, not just the subject matter in your curriculum. They come to you on a variety of skill levels. Meet the child where she is.

You must be understanding . . . if only you could walk in their shoes. Often your classroom is the most pleasant environment the student has all day. Make it a pleasant experience!

Reach out to each student. Make him feel that your interest in him is genuine. Spend time letting each one know that you care in spite of the circumstances. You must gain his trust. If they believe you care and trust your sincerity, they will learn—and shine—for you.

THE MIRACLE DIAMOND GEM

Louise Mikell

*My true story at Barnard Elementary School
in Washington, D.C.*

The afternoon was busy as usual, with the sixth graders completing assignments and practicing activities for the visit to the British Embassy, while I helped with selling potato chips for our fundraiser.

Finally, all activities were completed and everyone was ready to leave. We walked to the front of the building, said our goodbyes and I said hello to their parents.

Back in the classroom, I closed out my plans and set up for the next day's program. Then I checked through the room and went down the steps to stop at the office.

As I went out the door to be home with my family, I thought, "Let me do something exciting for our dinner."

While standing in line at the Safeway checkout, I thought about my daughter and her special science project. I thought, "I know she did well."

As I paid for and picked up my purchase in a hurry, my heart began to burn and dance. I stopped and stared at my finger. What?! The setting is empty! My diamond of 26 years is gone! Where is it? It's gone!

"No!" I yelled. I stood stunned. What?! How could this happen to me? "What did I do wrong?" I yelled again, "It's gone!"

My thoughts began to trace my day's movements. I got hot, nervous and shaky. Anger flared in my heart. "How could this happen to me?" I cried out again.

Well, it's gone! It's gone! It's just gone, I decided, as I tried to calm down.

Everything now ceased to be important. I didn't tell my husband or my daughter. I just got through the evening and prayed. I worried into the late night hours. "It's got to be at school! I couldn't lose that," I told myself. "What am I to do? Try to calm down and get over this disaster."

Back in a cleaned classroom the next morning, I went straight to the blackboard where I was selling chips. My heart was burning and beating fast again. I was afraid to look down, but intuition pushed me and I did!

Was that it, close to the wall, or a dust ball? No! It was shining! It was a miracle! It was my diamond hiding there all alone. I dared not touch it for fear that I would drop it and see it roll away. The masking tape! Where was the tape? I broke off a piece of tape, covered the stone dot and then picked it up.

I found it! I found it! My shiny bright gem was all dusty and grimy. By now, I was nervous and excited too. I yelled loudly, "I got it." I just stood still and rested. This was a miraculous happening of a lifetime, I thought.

"Thank you God for your grace," I prayed.

When I got home in the late afternoon, I showed my family the vacant ring setting and told them the story of the miracle of my shining *Diamond Gem*.

● ● ●

Sometimes we find children who are lost Gems. We take them as they are, dust them off, refine them, teach them, love them and testify that they were lost and now are found. Children—Miracle Gems!

Extraordinary School Moments 9/11/2001

Romaine B. Thomas

Unexpectedly, without any warning or indication, my entire school day was shattered, disrupted and changed from a calm, sunny morning to a chaotic state of affairs. The impact on Ketcham Elementary School, where I was Principal, was horrific and devastating. It was a day I will never forget: Tuesday, September 11, 2001.

On this particular day, which was just the beginning of a new school year, I started the morning with my usual routine of greeting students and parents as they happily marched into the lunchroom for breakfast. I continued with great enthusiasm and supervision of school entry. It was obvious that teachers had done a very good job of training the children on rules and procedures for a safe and orderly school environment.

As I walked through the halls and observed classes, I knew that the students and teachers were prepared for an exciting day. Ketcham School, a nearly one-hundred-year-old building, located just off the Anacostia River in Washington, D.C., was a safe haven for many of the children and their families. Survival was challenged by poor economic conditions, which sometimes created unwholesome living. Because of the dedication, compassion and commitment demonstrated by the school's staff, I had great confidence and faith in their abilities to carry out the mission and goals we had established for the school year, despite any obstacles faced by our students.

Administrators know that any day could be filled with adversities. These matters may require immediate attention and create additional demands upon the school day. This was exactly what took place on September 11, 2001.

Upon returning to my office with a great amount of satisfaction about being on target for the school year, I briefly reflected on the previous evening when I met with my fifth grade teacher James Debeuneure, his student Rodney Dickens, and Rodney's mother to discuss their departure for the next morning.

James Debeuneure was a fine example of the dedicated and special teacher with great compassion for his students. He was the father of two young adults. Rodney Dickens, the oldest son of a single mother, had several siblings. Rodney was an excellent student and highly talented. This would be a wonderful opportunity for him to extend his educational experiences. He eagerly looked forward with great expectation, pride and excitement to taking his first extended airplane trip away from his hometown, Washington, D.C.

Ketcham's teacher and student would join two other teams consisting of teacher Sarah Clarke and student Asia Cotton from Bertie Backus Middle School, and teacher Hilda Taylor and student Bernard Brown from Leckie Elementary School on an excursion led by Ann Judge and Joe Ferguson of the National Geographic Society. They were traveling to the Channel Islands National Marine Sanctuary off the coast of California for a scientific study project.

This was to be a culminating event for the District's Geographic Alliance to participate in a research project entitled the Sustainable Seas Expeditions. Working with an oceanographer, they would do fieldwork that included swimming, hiking and kayaking with marine biologists. This was such a wonderful opportunity for the teachers and especially the students to observe and learn firsthand about sea life and their habitats under and around the sea.

I was overjoyed that our team would be able to share their experiences with our staff and students when they returned. In the midst of thinking about this opportunity, I was suddenly interrupted by our reading teacher who came into the office and announced that her daughter had called with unsettling news about an airplane crashing into one of the twin towers at the World Trade Center in New York City. My office staff and I instinctively turned on the television. To our horror we witnessed the unbelievable scene of the airplane crashing into the World Trade Center. As we watched and listened to the news throughout the morning we became aware of the other crashes, the loss of lives, and horrific destruction.

With the news coverage of an airplane that had been hijacked by terrorists and crashed into the Pentagon, it became all too unreal and close to home. Then there was sickening and disheartening realization that our teachers and students were aboard Flight 77 that had hit the Pentagon. Unbelievably, we saw the flames leaping from one of the most secure buildings in the Washington Metropolitan Area and heard that a 75-foot-wide hole was made through the west wall. All hope of any survivors from the wreckage was lost.

Finally I managed to get a call through the tangle of busy signals to the airport authorities, only to confirm the fate of our beloved teachers, students and the kind and supportive staff of the *National Geographic*. This tragedy was too overwhelming to even comprehend.

As word of the tragedy moved through the school building and out into the community, some of the staff members and parents assembled into the office. Looking upon this scene, and disheartened, I needed to move into action to help keep this tragic situation under control.

Quickly, I ran over in my mind our school system's protocols for handling emergency situations and got key staff into position. I used the code system to alert the teachers and signal for students to be dismissed only to parents. Many parents had heard the unfolding news about the crashes around the country and reports of terrorism.

Parents were now filing into the building because employers were allowing their workers to leave for home. Streets were quickly filling up and massive traffic jams were occurring throughout the area—making it difficult for parents to get to the school.

As fear and concern spread, the mother of student Rodney Dickens came to the school to pick up her other children. I don't know how she came to realize that her own son, a bright and intelligent student, and his devoted teacher had been lost at the site of the Pentagon crash. But it was evident that she still had hope for their survival.

As teachers, staff, students and parents embraced her and gave her kind words of courage and hope, I moved forward to help her through the events of the day and to give her and her children privacy and support. All of our collective outpouring of compassion, expressions of caring, and the knowledge that our school community was now a part of a national tragedy gave way to somberness and remorse about the loss of Rodney and Mr. Debeuneure.

A decade after the events of September 11, 2001, this experience has renewed the spirit of thanksgiving and belief in humility of mankind. Finally, the sacrifice of the lives of Rodney Dickens and James Debeuneure, heroes from our own school, and those who were with them that day will always be with each and every member of the Ketcham School community.

● ● ●

Safety and security don't just happen; they are the result of collective consensus and public investment. We owe our children, the most vulnerable citizens in our society, a life free of violence and fear.

–Nelson Mandela
Former President of South Africa

THE JASON PROJECT

Sandra Britt Jenkins
District of Columbia Teacher of the Year
2004

As a science educator, I suspect my inspirations came early in life.

Two people closest to me provided the most inspirations and influence in my life: my grandmother and my mother. These two women gave me an opportunity to be the most curious youngster that I could be. My surroundings (a small town in southern Florida) afforded me the latitude for all kinds of explorations and pointed me in the teaching and learning direction.

I was sandwiched between two curious and active brothers whom I shadowed into wood and play areas. I went wherever they went. This was the beginning of my science career which had roots under my grandmother's house digging in the sand with my brothers for those little doodlebugs and mosquito larva which we counted.

Among my greatest accomplishments are the student project outcomes derived from such global learning opportunities like the Jason Project. The Jason Project is designed to link learning in the classroom and beyond. It encourages in-depth studies of selected environmental areas. Through this project, my students have traveled with their classmates to the Panama Rainforest, the Hawaii Islands, and the Bermuda Coral Reef.

These travel experiences and the resultant annual science fair energized my students and increased parental involvement at and beyond the local school level. The result was a recommitment to and increased investment in their children's educational careers. An additional accomplishment, one that was also most rewarding, involved one of my students in my science class. This student selected, researched and presented an award-winning science project at Stuart-Hobson Middle School that won city-wide recognition in the annual science fair—and an internship with a NASA scientist at the Goddard Space Flight Center.

Because of the passion that science can awaken in curious students, I see it as my task as a successful science teacher to keep encouraging young people to participate in research activities and opportunities. My greatest contribution is keeping alive the academic dream of science and acting as an advocate for middle schools in the District of Columbia Public School System.

I continue to select and plan professional development opportunities that identify and focus on additional science activities to capture the imagination of middle school students. For example, I conducted a presentation at the 2001 National Middle School Conference featuring the science pursuits of Stuart-Hobson Middle School. I presented these student projects to a national audience as an example of an outstanding middle school in the Washington Metropolitan Area.

EDUCATORS HAVE UP AND DOWN DAYS

Marie Richardson

Sometimes when I was teaching, and later carrying out my various duties as a librarian, I would have days when my spirits were down and I would be feeling a little discouraged about working with children who seemed not at all interested in learning. And then my thoughts would stray from the present moment to days long ago when I was a student. I would remember incidents from those days that had a positive impact on my life as a student. Then I would realize that I might not always know how much what I was doing for my students was making a difference in their lives. These thoughts would encourage me to keep trying even in difficult times.

Here is an example of a memory that lifted my spirits:

My parents moved our family to northeast Washington, D.C., in 1941. My brother and I had to attend a new school: Burrville Elementary School on Division Avenue and Hayes Street, Northeast. We lived at 54th and East Capitol Street and had to walk up the hill, down the hill and up the next hill to Burrville. As time went on, we began to look forward to our trip to and from school because the educational environment and teachers were so inviting and inspirational. It made our daily walk a joy.

Memories like this made me hope that some of my students were having similar experiences that I didn't know about. And I hoped that those experiences would give them pleasant memories when they looked back on their school days in which I played a part.

So I say to you who are still in the classroom or have other roles with our students today: be encouraged. You may never know the positive ways that you impact the lives of your students. They may never take time now to say, "Thank you." But they will remember you in later years with gratitude.

Little Child . . . I See The Africa In You, and I Learn!

Marion O. Williams

Little child,
I, your teacher,
yearn to provide for you
opportunities to see, learn, realize and discover
the heritage of your people in you . . .
heritage that has brightened your fire.

Little child, my learner,
allow me, please, to tap your friendliness
and borrow your creativity,
to be inspired by your energy and your charm
from your eternal fires
and see the Africa in you.

I, your teacher,
see the music when you speak
and the bounce in your stride,
see the flow of your nimble fingers
and the expressiveness of your hands.

I see the pride in your joyful walk,
I hear the bell tones of your laughter
and the richness of your voice.
The Africa in you cannot be denied.
I perceive it!

Little child,
I, your teacher, sense the patience in you,
thousands of years of persistence
and thousands of years of survival.

Child of my classroom,
Africa survives in your consciousness.
Your kinship to kings and princesses from afar
lives in your every act.

Little child,
may you know the gratitude and joy
I feel in teaching you.

Little child,
I thank you
for allowing me, your teacher,
to learn in your spirit.

WHY I BECAME A TEACHER

Cassandra Wilkins
4th Grade Teacher
Raymond Education Campus

There are many reasons why I became a teacher. The first and main one is that my mother was a teacher and taught for over 30 years before her death.

I continue to teach because of the love I have for the children. It is such a reward to have students come back and tell me how much of a difference I made in their lives.

The benefits of teaching can't be seen in what I drive or the house I live in, but by the time spent doing what I love to do the most: TEACH!

TEACH THE CHILDREN

Ermyn Roberts

Teach the children,
Teach them well!
Their minds are so pure and so free.
They seek our guidance, our knowledge, our skills.
Let us give in abundance, creating new choices,
Exploring what can be.

Teach the children,
Teach them well!
We must strive to reach their very core.
Our mission is urgent, our mission is clear,
Let us strive for excellence, soaring high,
Always expecting more.

Teach the children,
Teach them well!
They deserve our best; they deserve to be heard.
Let us continue to push, continue to teach.
Success for the children
Is success for the world.

WHEN TEACHERS INSPIRE

Ermyn Roberts

When teachers inspire,
Minds open and unravel,
Missing pieces are soon found,
Avenues of new possibilities widen,
Learning becomes real!

When teachers inspire,
Weak voices become strong,
Connections are made with conviction,
Stubborn frowns give way to glowing smiles,
Learning now lights the path, directs the journey!

When teachers inspire,
Ideas flow to novel creations,
Challenges become stepping stones to a goal,
Resistance slowly dissolves, replaced by determination,
Learning becomes the vital tool to success.

When teachers inspire!

AND THE CHILDREN SHALL CARRY ME BACK

Sandra Britt Jenkins

As I approach each new year, I have a greater sense of *urgency.*
I must be vigilant in my efforts to teach children how to learn and
properly prepare for a global society that requires authentic skills.
My teaching must take on greater depth and broader vision with
each new group of students.

Children must be enriched by challenging, progressive
experiences. The intensity of my commitment is deeply rooted in
the fear of what will happen to young people if we fail to develop
rigorous programs that encourage them to be life-long learners
who need to develop an educational thirst. It is truly a *survival issue*
for they must be a part of the *global mainstream.* The dividing line
today is not necessarily one of color, character, or background, but
one of education. This writer strongly believes that a young person's
quality of life will be directly linked to the level of knowledge,
problem solving techniques, and skill attainment. Further, I
believe that my investment and participation in continuous
professional development enables me to provide students with the
best curriculum/instruction, and that makes me an outstanding
educator.

Fundamentally, I believe that instruction for all children
begins with the children. We must teach students from their own
knowledge base, identifying their strengths and teaching them how
to learn and acquire new skills. Variety in teaching strategies, high

standards and expectations, and global exposure are critical teaching ingredients in the student improvement formula. Children must not only be introduced to a larger world but also involved in it in an interactive fashion.

This writer firmly believes that an outstanding teacher is a catalyst who offers interactive learning opportunities to teach students. Activities should be designed to increase environmental awareness, develop science literacy and open doors to a broad spectrum of continuous learning. Instruction and rewards are student outcomes that are both reinforcing and rewarding. My students reward me by developing environmental awareness, learning values through science application, becoming guardians and stewards of the environment, and making the world a better place via a heartfelt commitment to community service.

FOR ASPIRING EDUCATORS

Jacqueline S. Williams

An acrostic is a poem or series of lines in which certain letters, usually the first in each line, form a name, motto, or message when read in sequence. This acrostic combines the writer's words of advice with words of inspiration from noted educators, politicians and scholars.

E— EDUCATE yourself efficiently and effectively for
"education is a precondition to survival in America today."
–Marian Wright Edelman

D—DIVERSIFY by developing and using all your skills and talents because
"true happiness involves the full use of one's power and talents."
– John W. Gardner

U—UNLOCK deepest UNDERSTANDING of learning potential and human development because, in order to meet learning needs,
"the educator must believe in [his own potential] and the potential of his pupil, and employ all his art in seeking to bring his pupil to experience this power."

– Ellen Key

C—COMMUNICATE and connect with the minds of your students to confront
"with courage what we see that needs changing so that we may direct our youth to use their power toward good ends."
— Mary McLeod Bethune

A— ACCEPT what comes your way with active participation and
"meet it with courage and with the best you have to give."
— Eleanor Roosevelt

T— TRUST YOURSELF as you travel life's journey.
"Take life's steps with faith even when you don't see the whole staircase."
— Martin Luther King, Jr.

O—ORGANIZE your thoughts, your space, your behavior, activities so that, with such careful planning, you can
"hitch your wagon to something larger than yourself to realize your true potential."
— President Barack Obama

R— REACH for success through struggle—for
"success is not to be measured by the position one reaches in life as by the obstacles one overcomes and the strength one gains in the struggle."
— Booker T. Washington

S— SHAPE YOUR CHARACTER by making satisfying choices and
"striving to instill the same determination in those you teach and guide. In the long run, we shape our lives, and we shape ourselves. The process never ends until we die. And the choices we make are ultimately our responsibility."
— John W. Gardner

A WORLD OF DIFFERENCE

Minnie Holcomb

Blessed by the appreciation of students and parents, I've taught all over the globe—from Africa to Asia to America. Overseas, in the 1960s, American students from missionary, military, and State Department families attended U.S. Department of Defense schools. As the only African American teacher at the schools, with my son and daughter being the only black students and my husband, one of the few black State Department officers, I provided many students with their first close interaction with a black person, a fact of life leading to one of my most memorable and profound educational experiences.

In Taegu, Korea, where I taught third and fourth grade, Jeff, the son of an American colonel, was having problems adjusting to school and life in Korea. He was very shy and introverted, and his painful lack of self-esteem interfered with his learning potential. Each night, he called me to discuss his homework and the day's events, and, to everyone's surprise, began to open up. As he became more self-assured and outgoing, Jeff began to interact with other students and even to enjoy school. I was personally commended by the colonel. The entire family came to see us off the day we left Korea.

Teaching overseas was always an adventure. One of my students in Liberia, West Africa, brought a mongoose and a big snake to class for show-and-tell. No "humdrum" kittens and puppies for us! Fortunately, even when our family returned permanently to the States, I had another opportunity to travel overseas as an educator.

Using the abacus to teach math to my kindergartners, I received a grant from the Cafritz Foundation to visit schools in China. With elaborate tours of schools and classrooms, they treated me like a celebrity. The children were charming and polite, inviting me to share their morning exercises in their school courtyards. My Chinese guides took me everywhere, from the Forbidden City to the Great Wall. I returned to the States with unique memories and stories that I shared with my own wonderful students at Shepherd Elementary School in Washington.

No matter the country, I've cherished my students, my most precious teaching secret. It's rewarding when students I taught 15, 20, even 30 years ago still recognize me and greet me with great affection and respect, whispering those magic words every educator loves to hear—"You'll always be my favorite teacher!"

We may not make the salary of an investment banker, attain the fame of a movie star, or wield the power of a politician, but no other profession can compete with the enduring appreciation and growth of hundreds of children—the evidence that we've made a world of difference in their young lives and our future.

MOLDED BY ME!

Christine D. Easterling

I went to college to pursue my life's dream
—to become a great educator.
Worked hard in English, math, science, social studies
and student teaching internship, the greatest motivator.

Graduated, applied for a position, then chose a school,
And got ready to implement that Golden Rule.

On my first day in the classroom, in came their cute little faces,
Such laughter and eagerness as they found their places.

I wanted to mold them into whatever they wanted to be.
Just think—all of this molding would be done over and over by
me!

I was determined to educate well the students in my care that day.
To make them feel at home in their own little way.

I built a warm environment, mentored and nurtured them on my
vine.
Listened and looked for signs of trouble and oooooh, how much
did I find!

But I persevered the best I could to mold those young minds,
Carefully, meticulously following the curriculum under state
guidelines.

I taught in many ways—small group, lecture, role play, and
hands-on,
Such gratification watching them develop very much on their own.

With a warm, positive environment, my darlings would be molded
just right.
I taught the children, loved and cared for them, with all my
educational might.

I tried to be the best role model day to day.
Tried to build confidence and help them succeed along the way.

Sometimes I play the protector's role, looking for signs of trouble
to see;
Much of what they innocently did, even now, creates laughter in
me.

It's graduation and they're stepping to "War March of the Priests,"
you see;
I am proud that I became an educator—to witness all that molding
done by me!

GREAT MOMENTS IN TEACHING

Dr. Delore President

Throughout the years, I enjoyed teaching visual arts on many levels (pre-kindergarten to 12th grade). I was elated to see mystified pre-kindergarten and kindergarten students' reactions to innovative approaches to art lessons. Examples include their use of tempera paint to mix primary colors (red, yellow and blue) to form secondary colors, orange (red+yellow), green (yellow+blue), and purple (blue+red). They also used clay to shape objects of choice.

My great teaching experience included having students participate in art exhibits and contests. Many of my students received awards and recognition, including a visit to the White House.

I wrote various proposals that received funding, including Home Learning Activities, Nurturing Values in Relationship to Art for Successful Achievement, and Folder-Grams.

I became the second teacher in the District of Columbia Public School System to be awarded the National Freedom Foundation of Valley Forge Teacher's Medal.

PALINDROME

Emma J. Coates

A palindrome is a word, verse, sentence or number that reads the same backward as forward. It can serve as a teaching exercise.

Scene: Courtroom

Lawyer: Please tell the court your first and last names.
Girl: Anna Hannah

Lawyer: Who was present when your brother Bob committed the crime?
Girl: Lil' Sis . . . Mom . . . Dad . . . and Eve were present.

Lawyer: Your Honor, Eve is the family dog. When did it occur?
Girl: Noon

Lawyer: I see. Then Bob escaped in a car. What kind was it?
Girl: A Toyota

Lawyer: Why didn't you stop him? What did you think it was?
Girl: Gag

Lawyer: And how was he caught?
Girl: Radar

Lawyer: What do you think of your brother now, Madam?
Girl: Dud

Lawyer: Seriously, now, what do you think of his actions?
Girl: Bob Hannah sinned.

Underline each palindrome in the skit.
How many did you find? _____

Write your own palindromes:

_____
_____
_____
_____
_____

CINQUAINS

Emma J. Coates

A cinquain is a five-line stanza. It can serve as a vocabulary exercise. Each of these ten cinquains has a progressive number of words: one, two, three, four, and back to one.

- **Students**
- Cheerful, Happy
- Working and Playing
- Type, Read, Homework, Coursework
- Scholars

- **Secretary**
- Typing, Filing
- Interviewing, Answering Telephones
- Extremely Talented and Tolerant
- Flamboyant

- **Principal**
- Pleasant, Gentle
- Often Forewarning Students
- Exciting and Exhilarating Profession
- Leader

- **Teachers**
- Correcting Assignments
- Often Teaching Mathematics
- Writing on Chalk Boards
- Instructors

- **Baseball**
- Outfielder, Pitcher
- Running, Catching, Hitting
- Sliding onto Second Base
- Player

- **Teachers**
- Wonderful Citizens
- Creating Bulletin Boards
- Delighted When Pupils Behave
- People

- **School**
- Spacious, Beautiful
- Organized, Conducive, Resourceful
- Discipline, Instruct, Prepare, Educate
- Structure

- **Counselor**
- Investigating, Analyzing
- Listen, Correct, Talk
- Encourage, Promote, Endorse Children
- Therapist

- **Football**
- Offense, Defense
- Throwing, Running, Kicking
- Exciting, Strenuous Exercise Program
- Player

- **Friends**
- Amicable, Endearing
- Smiling, Laughing, Playing
- Exciting and Fun Conversations
- Acquaintances

Lunchtime!

Alberta H. Coleman

"What's on the menu? Can you smell it?"

"Spaghetti and meatballs. It smells good."

All the school children's eyes are on the food being served, carefully scooped, lifted and placed on each plate.

Lines are formed. Trays are picked up along with utensils and napkins. Served students carefully walk to assigned tables, place trays down, sit and quickly unwrap fork and spoon.

Meatballs are plump and tender, separate easily and are tasty. Sauce and spaghetti are flavorful. Children delve in with pleasure. The room is quiet. Everyone is busy eating in satisfaction.

Tasty turkey hot dogs with relish and mustard on warm buns are also delightful with warm mashed potatoes and corn. The food commands attention until it is totally consumed, leaving everyone contented.

Special holiday lunches replicate similar behavior: warm breast of turkey with light gravy, sweet potatoes, corn and green beans. All forks are busy and children relish the meal.

Meanwhile the brown baggers munch their lunch in relative silence:

"What do you have, Tommy?"

"Liverwurst and cheese with lettuce. And you?"

"Peanut butter sandwich and a banana. We don't have a turkey yet," says Susie.

"Try a little turkey," says Mary. "I can't eat all of this."

"Thanks, Mary!" They respond in unison as Mary spoons over two moist pieces of turkey.

"Let's come to order. Quiet down now!" the microphone commands.

They are ready for recess.

RECESS

Alberta H. Coleman

Memory fades, but we recall
    the most joyous time of the school day for all.
Out of the doors the children flew,
    oblivious to me and you.
From their lines so carefully formed,
    they suddenly decided to run.
Mouths opened wide as sounds come forth
    of joy, relief and onward mirth.

A race ensues as though by cue
    to the swings which were so few.
The first to reach, sit to claim,
    Then pump legs back and forth with aim.
Outbursts come without a name:
    "My turn next!" "Hurry Up!"
    "You wait your turn!" their voices exclaim.
Some pair to push and propel the swinger
    to hurry and bring their turn sooner.
Legs bend back, then forward,
    propelling the swings ever upward.
Swings go high toward the sky
    for views of things near and far.
Such deep breathing with each lift,
    soaring through the air is a super gift.

A circle has formed around
    the "merry-go-round."
In unison facing the same direction,
    runners push and push against traction.
Round and round circling faster,
    then all legs leap up and sit in satisfaction.
Circling, sitting, viewing the scene,
    smiles abound for all in glee.
Until slowing down, then all feet hit the ground
    to start over for another go-round.
Many sit going around and around
    as it spins upon the ground,
Giving a twirling sensation,
    circling while viewing the old school grounds.

Climbers are already
    on the "monkey bars."
Some are at the very top
    swinging from rung to rung;
    arms alternately reach as
    hands grasp the bars,
Across the top of the "jungle gym"
    or, as we say, the monkey bars.
Others are at the bottom
    safe and sound on a rung,
    bending at the waist,
    letting feet touch the ground.
Those in the middle
    climb through the bars
    either up, down or to the side,
    or hang with feet dangling down.
Eyes watch from below –
    the climbing, hanging, grasping,
    reaching and swinging.
Oh, what majestic movement and fun!

There's a line at the sliding board
   up the ladder all the way to the top.
One slides down, hands up, so fast,
   feet hit the ground with a ka-plop.
Another follows, sliding and holding,
   then hands up, and a slower stop.
The next one slides fast
   and then jumps off.
Back to the ladder, they all climb again
   for another grand slide down on one's behind
   until the bell sounds.

Swinging up and down;
Climbing a ladder to slide down;
Jumping on to spin around;
Climbing up to turn around or hang upside down;
Nothing beats fun on the
swings, slide, bars and merry-go-round.

Recess is the best time—the most joyous time!

INEXORABLE FORCES

Alberta Robinson Clêment

Dear Lord,

We, the members of the District of Columbia Retired Educators Association, need Your Holy Guidance as we proclaim to pass on the torch to our successors.

> Beginning with a heart of Selflessness,
> Moving carefully toward Thankfulness,
> And escalating toward Thoughtfulness.

Our mentors have taught us important lessons:

Selflessness allows us to spend tireless hours helping others.

Thankfulness is the rewarding inheritance of mentors who guided us toward higher planes of learning and dedication.

Thoughtfulness is our special reward from the example of Jesus' love.

Thus, we are thankful for these guiding forces which have ignited and boosted our inner spirit, enabling us to PUSH!

> **P**ersevering onward.
> **U**niting our forces.
> **S**trengthening all bonds.
> **H**eralding the victory!

A TEACHER'S PRAYER

Alberta Robinson Clêment

Dear Heavenly Father,

I am thankful for the unrelenting, caring educators who marched through the years, nourishing the minds of our youth with a hunger to "learn to live and live to learn."

We know that our battle is not completed. We must persevere and pass this inner strength to educators who follow in our footsteps.

Again, Heavenly Father, we ask that you empower us with the strength and courage to move forward to accomplish our united aim.

Amen.

Students' Expressions of Praise

RAYMOND EDUCATION CAMPUS

GRADES 2 THROUGH 7
WASHINGTON, D.C.

James Alleyne

My Favorite Teacher Ever

She is nice and she is loving. She gives you things if you are good. She is my favorite teacher ever. She is the nicest teacher. These are great experiences in school, making friends and having a nice teacher.

Kamara D. Anthony

Teachers R Unique

Teachers are very nice.

Teachers are unique in their very own way, in math, reading, social studies and other subjects.

I can be unique when a teacher teaches me how to get A's instead of C's, D's or F's because she wants me to be unique.

That's why teachers R unique.

When I think of myself I'm being unique.

When my teacher looks at me I am unique.

Teachers R unique because each and every day they teach me. Unique, unique, unique.

When teachers get angry "huh" they're angry in their own way.

Which makes them unique.

When teachers give A's they give them in their own ways.

That's why they are very, very unique.

I am too because they taught me how to be unique.

Chris Ataito

Thank You to My Teacher

You have helped me with a lot of things. I know the reason you get a little upset at us because you want us to give our attention and focus. Deep down in your heart, I know that you love us. You want us to grow up to be smart and also you want us to know what's wrong and what's right. You give us good choices to make. Thank you for being an outstanding teacher.

Jennifer Berrios

I Will Not Forget My Teacher

My teacher is a nice teacher.
She helps kids learn.
She is the greatest teacher ever.
She plays fun games.
Who will ever forget her?
I will not forget her.
Because she is the best teacher ever!

Tanaye Bridges

Teachers Are Nice (Haiku)

You are nice to me
You are the best teacher ever!
I love you so much

Editor's note: A "haiku" is an unrhymed Japanese lyric poem with a fixed three-line form consisting of 5, 7, and 5 syllables respectively.

Jose Burruca

I Love My Teacher

I love my teacher like a muffin,
I love her like a rose.
I love my teacher like a flower about to come out of hearts.
I love you like a butterfly

Carlos Calles

Thank You Beautiful Teacher

Beautiful teacher
Helps me with all subjects.
Thank you for teaching.

Shaira Corona

A Letter to My Teacher

Dear Teacher,

You make me feel like I am at home. Other times you make me feel like I am in huge trouble. I love you, but I think you should be patient with me. You are a pretty teacher, and I like to see you happy.

Aisha Djibo-Noma

They Do Great Things for Me

Teachers and staff members do all these great things for me and others.

I will explain why I love my teachers.

They give me respect.

They are fun.

They are nice, and they are unique.

For example, my Spanish teacher made a suduko out of adjectives in Spanish. And my math teacher takes us skiing ever year and tells us it's fun and helps with math like angles and how many mph that we go.

I also like my history teacher. He puts history words in Jeopardy in some type of amazing way.

I really like my principal because without her we wouldn't get our field trips approved, and also without her, I wouldn't be able to enjoy soccer and other things I'm into.

I can't forget my other favorite teachers like my science teacher.

This is why I love my teachers and other educators. I want to give a shout out for my aftercare teacher for being there for me.

Peace!

Jermaine Evans

All the Things I Like
About My Teachers

I like my teachers because they are nice.
They help us learn new things.
They help us deal with other people when things go wrong.
They try to keep us out of trouble.
They give us things for being good.
That's what I like about my teachers.

Dootiny Herdrichs

A Rap for My Teachers

I love my teacher.
I got good teachers.
My favorite subject is Math.
I got a very crazy laugh.
When I come to school, I feel . . . PROUD!
We eat, breakfast, lunch and . . . Snack.
When I play outside, I'm very eager and LOUD!
All of these are not opinions, they are facts.
I love to learn, and be smart.
I am respectful, responsible and ready every day. All day!
I'm very creative.
I get to school on time.
I eat limes and lemons.
I got a bunny and I'm very funny!
I wear a bun . . . I'M DONE!

Angelica Hernandez

The Meaning of Teacher

T—Try
E—Excellent
A—At work
C—Come on time.
H—Happy
E—Elegant
R—Ready

Junior Hernandez

My Two Favorite Teachers

My favorite teacher gives us parties and she gives tiger paws a lot of times.

My other favorite teacher gives candy to kids who behave like adults.

Mykia Johnson

All About My Teacher

My teacher is very nice
but sometimes uptight.
She loves us all in a very equal way.
My teacher may yell
but at the end of the day it wouldn't matter.
My teacher teaches me everything.
Everything I need to know.
My teacher could be cool.
My teacher could be angry
but it still wouldn't matter.
My parents may teach me manners and words
but my teacher teaches me knowledge,
knowledge that can get me a great job.
I love my teachers always
but when I go to another school they will be like no other.

Antoine Jones

Rap For My Teachers
Because . . . Because . . .

These are my favorite teacher because because because.
They teach me how to play basketball.
They teach me how to play football.
They teach me how to do math and free style.
They teach me how to box.
They teach me how to use computers.
They teach me how to write essays, raps, and poems.

Zariah Lochman

I Love My Teacher

Funny, loving,
Beautiful, smart, kind teacher
I love you so much.

Cesar Lopez

Thank You for Teaching Me

I am happy that I am in your class because I know that you will teach a lot of things like math and reading. You are funny and pretty. I was glad when we had pizza and an ice cream party. You are the best teacher. Thank you for teaching me.

Jationa Lopez

My Rap for Teachers
t . . . t . . . t . . . Teachers

Teachers teachers t . . . t . . . t . . . teachers
help me learn new things.

The teachers teachers
are nice and cool.

Teachers t . . . t . . . t . . . teachers
help me on my work.

All of the teachers
help all of the students.

The best teachers, teachers
t . . . t . . . t . . . are mine.

Teachers Teachers t . . . t . . . t . . . Teachers
all of the teachers are fun, cool, and helpful.

Daysi Madrid

What I Want to Learn

Will you teach me how to read? Can you teach me how to round? There are a lot of things I want to learn.

Why I Would Like to Be a Teacher

The reason I would like to be a teacher is because all the children in the world will learn a lot. We will teach them reading, math, social studies, and science.

Cheria Marphy

My Loving Teacher

You are the best! You help me so much with my reading, math, social studies, and science. I love you so much like my mother. Thank you for everything, Thank you for the pizza and treats too. You are the best! I hope you love me like I love you.

Steven Medreano

My Teacher Gets Me Ready

I thank you for teaching me in fourth grade to get ready for fifth grade.

It won't be easy. I will work hard. You were always responsible, funny and sometimes you get serious but you're still a good teacher. I wish you luck in your job and have a good year of teaching and learning.

Ashley Mejia

My Smart Teacher

I love you,
I hug you,
I kiss you,
I'm looking at a smart, awesome teacher.
She is from D.C.
Guess who is this teacher?
Maybe it can be you.

Anthony Mendoza

My Teacher Is Like a Butterfly

You are as nice as a butterfly.
You are as sweet as candy.
You help like an assistant.
You wear different colors like a rainbow.

Imani Mills

My Teacher Is So Pretty

You are so pretty.
You smell good and dress pretty.
You are sweet and good.
Guess who wrote this.

Mamalee Milton

You Are the Best

I feel happy when I am around you. You are the best teacher! I love you, and I remember how you used to make funny things and be funny. You gave us a pizza party. I remember when I first came to this school and I told you my name, you started singing my song.

Zanaya Pannell

What Teachers Are

T-houghtful
E-ducational
A-mazing
C-areful
H-elpful
E-xcellent
R-espectful
S-mart

Nysiah Lowery-Parks

What the Word Teacher Means

T—to teach
E—education
A—attend
C—class
H—hearing
E—excellent
R—ready

Luis Lima Sandoval

My Acrostic for Teachers

T-Try
e-excellent
a-advance
c-class
h-hearing
e-education
r-responsible

Chrishon Spencer

My Teacher Does Good Things

My teacher is a lady with brown hair.
My teacher is good with her math and reading.
She helps the homeless.
She helps the people who need it.

Maria Velasquez

Why I Like My Teachers

I like my teachers because
They are cool.
They don't act rude.
I learn new things.
When I have an idea my brain goes bing.
My teachers are great.
They don't hate.
My teachers are my inspiration.
They are like my role models.
I get my education from them.
I will always respect them.
Even when I'm in a bad mood,
I will always be respectful,
responsible and ready when
It comes to school
I believe I could do anything
with the help of my teachers,
principals and friends.

ABOUT THE AUTHORS

(EDUCATORS)

Frances Anne Green Clarke is a native of Durham, N.C. She received both her BA and MA degrees in French/English from North Carolina Central University. This 41-year veteran teacher was a four-time *Who's Who Among America's Teachers* and had over 35 essay/oratorical contest winners in the District of Columbia. She retired from Calvin Coolidge High School and enjoys writing.

Alberta Robinson Clément holds a B.A. from Wayne State University and an M.S. from Michigan State University. She taught English in Lansing, Michigan prior to teaching in Washington, D.C. She has served as curriculum writer, coordinator, administrator, community liaison, educational consultant and school SGA/newspaper advisor. Her students have won many local and national poetry, oratorical and writing contests.

Emma J. Coates, program chairperson for DCREA, is a native of Fayetteville, N.C. She received her Master of Education in Reading from Trinity College in Washington, D.C. Coates was a classroom teacher, coordinator of the gifted and talented program, and building resource teacher at Katie C. Lewis ES in Northwest Washington. She retired from Evans MS as the instructional facilitator, and enjoys reading and traveling.

Alberta H. Coleman is a member of the DCREA Book Writing Club. She has B.S. and M.A. degrees in Education from Eastern Michigan University and the University of Michigan respectively. Mrs. Coleman has taught school children in the states of Michigan, Minnesota, Maryland, and the District of Columbia, and is now retired.

Christine D. Easterling is president of the District of Columbia Retired Educators Association, Inc. She also served as vice president. She is a native of Blackstone, Virginia. She earned her M.A. degree from Howard University in Public School Administration and M.A. degree from the University of the District of Columbia in

Curriculum Development. She also earned a B.S. degree in Business Education from St. Paul's Episcopal College.

Through the years, she has been honored as State Vice-Principal of the Year by The National Association of School Administrators, Teacher of the Year by The National Education Association, Soror of the Year Award of Theta Omega Omega Chapter, Alpha Kappa Alpha Sorority, Inc., and Outstanding Ward 4 Educator by the District of Columbia Board of Education.

Christine has been the recipient of the Youth Service Award, Xi Zeta Omega Chapter, Alpha Kappa Alpha Sorority, Inc.; President's Medal for Outstanding Teaching by Trinity College; Meritorious Service Award for Outstanding Leadership in Education, Montfort Point Marine Association; Congratulatory Educators Award by Maryland Congresswoman Constance Morella; New Member of the Year Award by Phi Delta Kappa, Howard University; and D.C. Public Schools Superintendent's Special Commendation Award for Outstanding Innovation in Technology.

Dr. Phyllis J. Hobson holds her Bachelor of Arts from Howard University, Master of Arts from American University, and doctorate from George Washington University. She served a 38-year career in the District of Columbia Public Schools as teacher, counselor and administrator. Dr. Hobson provided professional and community service as a member and officer in the Alpha Kappa Alpha Sorority, Inc., the Coalition of 100 Black Women, the Howard University Women's Club, and the District of Columbia Retired Educators Association (DCREA). She served as President of DCREA for two terms, 2004-2006 and 2008-2010.

Minnie Irby Holcomb – aka "the Diva" – is a retired elementary school teacher who has taught in the United States and abroad. Born and raised in Laurens, South Carolina, Minnie is a proud graduate of Sanders High School and Tuskegee University.

Minnie's teaching career started early. As her siblings will attest, she was a high-energy child who always took charge of a room and loved to perform in front of an audience.

Today, Minnie serves on the boards of the DCREA and the D.C. Boys Choir, and is an active member of the Alpha Wives of Montgomery County and the Young, Active Christians Club of Shiloh Baptist Church.

One of Minnie's greatest joys is being recognized and greeted with love and affection by her many former students.

Sandra Britt Jenkins, 2004 District of Columbia Teacher of the Year, holds a Master's in Interdisciplinary Studies from National Louis University. She has taught in New Jersey, Nicosia, Cyprus and Okinawa, Japan. Her teaching traveling experiences includes Bermuda, Hawaii and Panama. After 41 years of teaching, she retired in 2010 and enjoys spending time with her grandson, William Jagan.

Constance T. Laws (Connie) served 39 years in D.C. Public Schools as a teacher, principal and central office administrator. She received her Bachelor of Science at D.C. Teachers College and her Master of Science at The George Washington University. In addition, she has completed scores of graduate hours in supervision and administration at Howard University, American University, University of Maryland, and Trinity University. A lover of poetry, Connie has written more than 300 poems on a variety of subjects. She is a life member of numerous professional organizations.

Louise M. Mikell is the archivist for DCREA. She was a sixth grade teacher at Barnard ES in Washington from 1965 to 1994. Louise was also teacher of grade six at Charles R. Drew ES. She holds a Master of Arts in Education and Teaching Teachers from The George Washington University. She obtained her undergraduate degree in English and history from Morgan State University in Baltimore, MD. She retired from Barnard ES in 1994.

Dr. Delore President, a well respected, innovative educator, believes all children can learn. She also believes that schools must prepare students to compete in a global economy. She earned her Bachelor of Arts in Education and Art from Howard University, Master of Arts in Education and Art from Goddard College (Plainfield, Vermont), and Ph.D. in Supervision and Administration from Union Institute and University (Cincinnati, Ohio). Her dissertation was entitled "Increasing Reading Scores of Third Graders Through Infusion of Visual Arts and Literacy." She has successfully developed and tested individually designed programs of studies in innovative education and art.

Marie Corbin Richardson taught English and social studies in junior high school before teaching in the elementary school. Later in her teaching career she became an elementary school Librarian. These educational experiences increased her desire to encourage students to read and enjoy the companionship of printed words. She obtained her undergraduate and graduate degrees from the University of Michigan. She retired from the Washington, D.C. school system and is an active member of the District of Columbia Retired Educators Association.

Ermyn Roberts is a retired D.C. Public Schools educator. She taught for 36 years at Janney Elementary School. She also worked as the resident mentor teacher at Janney for several years. In her retirement, she continues to work with students by volunteering as a reading tutor in her community. In her spare time, she enjoys reading, writing poems, singing, and traveling.

William Henry Simons was president of the Washington Teachers Union for 25 years. A native of Washington, he graduated from Dunbar High School in 1940. He saw military service in Europe during World War II, reaching the rank of sergeant major in the 262nd Quartermaster Battalion and receiving the Bronze Star and the Croix de Guerre. After earning a B.S. degree from the historically black Miner Teachers College (later the District of Columbia Teachers College) in 1947, he began teaching social studies at Banneker Junior High School. In 1949 he acquired a master's degree from New York University and later held fellowships from Howard University and the City University of New York.

Shirley A. Smith earned her Bachelor of Science in Mathematics and Master of Education from Howard University. She holds the Masters plus 60 hours toward the Ed.D. from The George Washington University.

Shirley's career of teaching mathematics at the secondary level includes public schools in Washington, D.C.; Detroit, Michigan; Cleveland, Ohio; Baltimore, Maryland, and Silver Spring, Maryland. She retired from the District of Columbia Public School System in 1998, followed by twelve years at Springbrook High School in Montgomery County, Maryland. In 2010, with over forty years of fulfilling and enjoyable teaching, she retired from the profession. She is a member of the National Council of Teachers of Mathematics, National Council of Supervisors of Mathematics, D.C. Council of Teachers of Mathematics, and Maryland Council of Teachers of Mathematics. She serves DCREA as chair of the Advocacy Committee and Travel Committee.

Romaine B. Thomas has devoted most of her life to education and community service. She is a highly respected career educator, classroom teacher, school principal and administrator in education circles and the community for outstanding achievements and accomplishments.

She served for over 25 years as the principal of John Henry Ketcham Elementary School, located in the Anacostia neighborhood of Washington. While providing outstanding leadership to the staff, children and parents, she successfully promoted school effectiveness and increased community involvement.

Romaine was one of 54 principals selected from across the nation and overseas to receive the National Association of

Elementary School Principals (NAESP) Distinguished Principals Award in 1984 from the U.S. Department of Education.

She received her Bachelor of Science from Miner Teachers' College (University of the District of Columbia) and Master of Education in Administration from The George Washington University. She also attended Temple University, Howard University, College of William and Mary, and Vanderbilt University for advanced study.

Cassandra Wilkins currently teaches fourth grade at Raymond Education Campus, where she has been for 19 years of her 21 years in teaching. She has also taught first grade and fifth grade. She obtained her undergraduate degree and master's degree (in Reading Education) from Bowie State College. She looks forward to teaching at the college level to prepare future teachers.

Jacqueline Smith Williams, a retired teacher and principal of the D.C. Public Schools, also retired from the positions as Director of HAP (Higher Achievement Program) and the Horning Brothers Learning Centers. She is a native Washingtonian, educated in the public schools. She began her love of books, reading and writing while spending hours in the neighborhood public library.

Jackie – as she is better known – is a graduate of Dunbar High School, Miner Teachers College and The George Washington University. Her membership in two book clubs and the DCREA Book Writing Club provides her with many opportunities to enjoy her favorite hobbies: reading and creative writing. Her writings include study guides for her bible study classes, dramas and readings for adults and children, biographies, tributes, and articles for social groups, her sororities (AKA and the National Sorority of Phi Delta Kappa, Inc.), and church journals. She is compiling articles from her personal journal and completing her memoir. Her favorite pastime is organizing and enjoying after-school book clubs with students in local public schools and sharing with them the enjoyment of reading. Her husband, daughter, and granddaughter (a budding writer) share her love of reading and creative writing.

Marion O. Williams, a native Washingtonian, is a retired District of Columbia Public School teacher. She is a poet, tutor and volunteer in public schools. She has travelled the world and made many international friends through the peace organization, U.S. Servas, Inc. She has spoken at conferences sponsored by the National Council of English Teachers and other educational organizations.

Marion is the author of a book of poetry, *Waiting for a Dream,* and plans to publish a second edition of poetry and short stories.

EPILOGUE

EDUCATORS MADE PRESIDENT OBAMA WHAT HE IS TODAY

President Barack H. Obama knows the value of educators and just how much they should be appreciated. Educators prepared and directed him to lead a fulfilling life that goes beyond a successful career, all the way to the Presidency of the United States of America.

In an address to a town hall meeting, President Obama said, "If our students lack the education they need, we will not succeed as a nation."

President Obama, who was born in Honolulu, Hawaii, on August 4, 1961, has led a life filled with exceptional education and a continuing commitment to serving others. He obtained his early education in Jakarta, Indonesia, and in Hawaii; continued his education at Occidental College in Los Angeles; received a B.A. in 1983 from Columbia University in New York; worked as a community organizer in Chicago; and studied law at Harvard University in Boston, where he became the first African American president of the *Harvard Law Review* and received a J.D. in 1991.

He then became an educator himself, teaching constitutional law at the University of Chicago. From 1997 to 2004, he served as a member of the Illinois State Senate. In 2004, he was elected as a Democrat to the U.S. Senate, where he served from January 3, 2005, to November 16, 2008. He was elected the 44th President of the United States on November 4, 2008, and was inaugurated on January 20, 2009.

Teachers were instrumental in laying the foundation stone of President Obama's life. His preschool teachers played major roles in his early development and in nurturing his young mind. Little did they know that they were helping to shape the life of a future president of the country! His teachers contributed to the shaping of his generation and future generations. They got the chance to befriend children, be their source of inspiration, win their hearts, and guide them through their journeys of life.

All of the educators in President Obama's life helped to instill the moral and ethical values he uses every day in the White House. His teachers developed his basic learning skills and were his academic role models. He derived inspiration from them. They enabled him to leave school with a whole lot of dreams and aspirations about his life outside the school and take them to the White House.

What if the President had had no TEACHERS? His life would have been a sad one without his teachers—and his parents and grandparents. I am sure he would say a special "thank you" to his teachers who gave their time and energy to make our country a better place.

Teachers and other educators acted as facilitators, incorporating and encouraging intellectual and social development in the President's formative years. As a student, he came up with questions and received answers. His teachers possessed thorough knowledge of their subjects and presented that knowledge effectively. They helped him find new things to explore. They helped to build alertness and precision in his expression.

Principals also played a major role in the President's development. They interacted with his parents, teachers and others affecting his life.

When he matriculated to the university, President Obama's professors guided his research and activities. They provided him with professional training for high-level jobs as well as for the development of his personality. The professors increased his body of theoretical knowledge as well as application to practical problems like the ones he faced as a community activist, Senator and now President.

The President, Vice President and Cabinet Members— Secretary of State, Secretary of the Treasury, Secretary of Defense, Attorney General, Secretary of the Interior, Secretary of Agriculture, Secretary of Commerce, Secretary of Labor, Secretary of Health and Human Services, Secretary of Housing and Urban Development, Secretary of Transportation, Secretary of Energy, Secretary of Education, Secretary of Veterans Affairs, Secretary of Homeland Security, White House Chief of Staff—all need to thank educators for shaping a better world for them.

It's time to write that thank-you letter to YOUR teachers, for it is your teachers who empowered you with the knowledge to take on the world!

Christine D. Easterling
President
District of Columbia Retired
Educators Association, Inc.

NOTES

NOTES